Nutrition

A Passion for Proteins

Kristin Petrie

ABDO
Publishing Company

visit us at
www.abdopub.com

Published by ABDO Publishing Company, 4940 Viking Drive, Edina, Minnesota 55435.
Copyright © 2004 by Abdo Consulting Group, Inc. International copyrights reserved in all countries. No part of this book may be reproduced in any form without written permission from the publisher.

Printed in the United States.

Cover Photo: Corbis
Interior Photos: Corbis pp. 1, 5, 6, 7, 8, 11, 12, 13, 14, 15, 17, 18, 21, 22-23, 24-25, 27, 28;
    U.S. Department of Agriculture and U.S. Department of Health and Human Services p. 29

Editors: Kate A. Conley, Stephanie Hedlund, Kristianne E. Vieregger
Art Direction: Neil Klinepier

Library of Congress Cataloging-in-Publication Data

Petrie, Kristin, 1970-
    A passion for proteins / Kristin Petrie.
        p. cm. -- (Nutrition)
    Summary: Describes the importance of proteins in the human body, types of foods that provide this nutrient, and how the body uses proteins.
    Includes bibliographical references and index.
    ISBN 1-59197-405-4
    1. Proteins in human nutrition--Juvenile literature. [1. Proteins. 2. Nutrition.] I. Title.

QP551.P3973 2003
613.2'82--dc21
                                                        2002043621

Contents

Proteins

Steak, eggs, hamburgers, hot dogs, chicken, milk, and cheese—what **nutrient** are we talking about? Protein! These foods are good sources of protein. They can be found in the milk and meat groups of the **Food Guide Pyramid**.

What else comes to mind when you think of protein? Muscles? How about Arnold Schwarzenegger? Protein plays an important role in building muscles. But, it also has many other important functions.

Protein is found in every cell of your body. In fact, the word *protein* comes from a Greek word that means "primary," or "most important." Protein is everywhere, so let's learn more about it.

Protein Power

Protein helps build muscle. Many people used to think that eating a lot of protein would help develop large muscles. Body builders used to eat raw eggs to increase their muscle mass. Now we know that a balanced diet and exercise are needed to develop muscles.

Arnold Schwarzenegger (standing) flexes his muscles, which protein helped develop.

Protein-Rich Foods

Peas are legumes. They hold their seeds in pods.

Protein is found in both animal- and plant-based foods. Animal-based foods include fish, meat, eggs, cheese, and milk. They are rich, concentrated sources of protein.

Some plant-based foods, such as beans and nuts, have more protein than meats. In plants, protein is most concentrated in the part of the plant that sprouts and grows. Legumes, or beans that keep their seeds in pods, are packed with protein. Some examples of legumes are peas, peanuts, chickpeas, lentils, black beans, and red beans.

You now know some foods that are important sources of protein. But, did you know protein also comes from less obvious sources? In fact, there is a little protein in nearly every food. Even a banana has one gram of protein!

Protein Values of Common Foods

High-Protein Foods	Protein in Grams
Chicken, 3$\frac{1}{2}$ ounces, light meat, roasted	31
Cottage cheese, 1 cup	26
Beef, extra lean, baked, 3$\frac{1}{2}$ ounces	23
Tuna, white, drained, 3 ounces	23
Lentils, cooked, 1 cup	18
Garbanzo beans, cooked, 1 cup	12
Tofu, raw, $\frac{1}{2}$ cup	10
Peanut butter, 2 tablespoons	9
Milk, any type, 1 cup	8
Yogurt, any type, 1 cup	8
Wheat germ, $\frac{1}{4}$ cup	7
Egg, 1 large	6
Rice, cooked, long grain, 1 cup	6
Cheese, hard, 1 ounce	6

Even this lobster contains protein!

Structure

Let's take our microscope and see what protein really looks like. If you take apart a single protein molecule, you get **amino acids**. Break down those amino acids and you are left with the **elements** carbon, hydrogen, oxygen, and nitrogen.

An even closer look reveals four groups in each amino acid. All groups are connected to a central carbon. The amino group is one nitrogen and two hydrogens clumped together. The acid group is one carbon, one hydrogen, and two oxygens clumped together. The last two groups are a single hydrogen and a side chain, which differs in each protein.

This example of a protein molecule was produced by a computer to show the different twists and turns that are possible.

Now it's time to put the protein molecule back together! First, the four groups join to form an **amino acid**. Then, the amino acid connects to other amino acids with the help of **peptide bonds**. They make amino acid chains called **polypeptides**. Finally, the polypeptides connect to form proteins.

Amino acid chains join in many ways. In fact, there are so many possible amino acid and peptide combinations that they can make thousands of different proteins! Some formations are simple chains. Others look like balls or baskets, letters of the alphabet, or crazy jungle gyms.

An Amino Acid

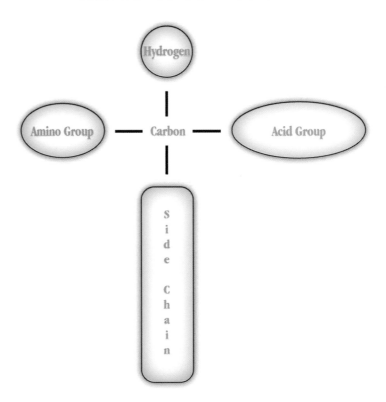

Amino Acids

Scientists have identified 20 different **amino acids**. Your body needs and uses all 20. They build your body's proteins.

Eleven of the amino acids are called nonessential amino acids. But, don't be fooled by their name—nonessential amino acids are still crucial! They are called nonessential because your liver makes them from chemicals in your body. Therefore, it is nonessential for you to seek them out in food.

The remaining nine amino acids are called essential amino acids. They must come from food. No matter how hard your body tries, it cannot make them. That's why eating foods with protein is important.

Protein-rich foods give your body the amino acids it needs.

Essential Amino Acids	Nonessential Amino Acids
Histidine	Alanine
Isoleucine	Arginine
Leucine	Asparagine
Lysine	Aspartic acid
Methionine	Cysteine (cystine)*
Phenylalanine	Glutamic acid
Threonine	Glutamine
Tryptophan	Glycine
Valine	Proline
	Serine
	Tyrosine*

* These are made by the body from essential amino acids in food. If the essential amino acids are not supplied, they can't be made and must come entirely from food.

The essential amino acids can be found in meat, eggs, cheese, and nuts.

Complete Proteins

Some proteins are composed of the right amounts of all nine essential **amino acids**. They are called complete proteins. The protein-rich foods that most easily pop into your head, such as meat, fish, and eggs, are complete proteins. Other complete proteins include dairy products such as cheese, milk, cream, and yogurt.

A few plant-based foods are complete proteins as well. For example, tofu and other soybean products contain all the essential amino acids. Most plant-based foods, however, are not complete. They are either missing some essential amino acids or have a smaller number of them.

Soybeans and tofu

Protein is important for all family members.

People who do not eat meat or dairy products can still receive enough essential and nonessential **amino acids**. To do this, they must eat a variety of plant-based foods. For example, they can eat fruits, nuts, and grains at one meal. At another meal, they can eat vegetables and legumes. Over time, their bodies will combine these essential amino acids to make complete proteins.

Children are an important exception to this kind of diet. That's because a large amount of vegetables and grains are needed to get all your essential amino acids. It may be more than your stomach can handle! Therefore, it is good for children to at least occasionally eat foods with complete proteins, such as eggs.

Eggs provide complete proteins.

Protein can help you
do well in sports
and in school!

Protein's Jobs

Every cell in your body contains protein. For that reason alone, it is very important. But, why else do you need protein? Let's investigate all of the jobs that protein does in your body!

Protein's biggest job is to build, maintain, and repair your body's **tissues**. Has anyone mentioned how much you've grown? Did that scrape on your elbow heal and disappear? Do your fingernails need to be cut, again? If so, you can thank protein! Proteins such as keratin and collagen are responsible for growing, repairing, and strengthening all of your bones, muscles, and other tissues.

Proteins have other jobs, too. Some proteins specialize in transporting substances in the blood. Hemoglobin is a good example of this. It carries oxygen to every part of your body. Other proteins move **nutrients** into and out of your body's cells. The protein that pumps sodium and potassium into and out of your cells helps your **nerves** work. This allows you to think and act!

Protein helps heal cuts, scrapes, and broken bones.

Some proteins have the job of being messengers. For example, insulin and thyroid proteins tell your body when you need more energy, and when you can save it for later. Antibodies are proteins that protect the body from **viruses** and bacteria. This helps you avoid colds and other illnesses.

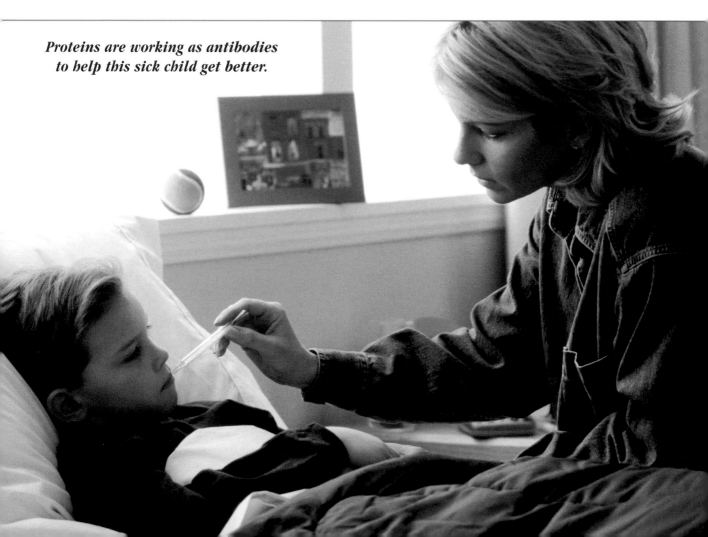

Proteins are working as antibodies to help this sick child get better.

Some proteins help chemical **reactions** take place. These proteins are called enzymes. Enzymes have a million functions, starting with breaking down the food that you eat. Protein **digestion** produces **amino acids** that may be put together in new formations. These new proteins may become enzymes themselves! They can help you breathe, see, and react.

Protein can also provide your body with energy. The body works best when its energy comes from carbohydrates. If there are not enough carbohydrates available, however, your body will use protein for energy. Muscle proteins and enzyme proteins are broken down into energy. This takes protein away from performing its normal functions in the body.

Enzyme Reproduction

There are thousands of protein enzymes building and changing inside of you right now. During digestion, enzymes break down food, and are themselves being broken down and rebuilt. This means there are many different types of enzymes performing various jobs in your body.

Digestion

Have you ever wondered what happened to the hamburger you ate for lunch? How did it turn into brain cells, the skin covering your fingers, or the muscle of your arms? The answers to these questions can be found by looking at how your body **digests** protein.

First, food proteins are broken down by your digestive system. In the stomach, acid changes the protein chain. This allows enzymes from the stomach, intestine, and pancreas to break down the protein. The small parts are absorbed into cells and then further broken down into **amino acids**.

Amino acids then enter a vein and travel to the liver. The liver determines how the amino acids will be used. It either distributes them throughout the body or breaks them down for energy.

Opposite page: It can be fun to include protein in your diet!

The **amino acids** that leave the liver go to the cells that need them. In those cells, the amino acids combine once again in new formations. Then they take care of all their important jobs.

How Much Protein?

How much protein do you need? Protein requirements vary with age. You are growing right now, so your body is using protein nonstop. With so much to do, it may seem as though you should eat tons and tons of protein.

A little bit of protein, however, goes a long way. As a growing, young person you need just 15 percent of your food to come from protein sources. That's because your body takes food proteins and makes nonessential **amino acids**.

It's quite easy to get the protein your body needs. In fact, the average American eats nearly twice the needed amount of protein each day! As you now know, a bit of protein can be found in nearly every food. So, it adds up quickly.

For example, a small hamburger at lunch and chicken or fish at supper easily adds up to around 50 grams of high-quality protein. That's nearly twice the amount you need. And, that doesn't even count the protein that came from snacks and the other foods eaten at your meals!

Even people who don't eat meat can reach their protein needs quickly. For example, for breakfast, you could eat one cup of cereal with one cup of milk. Together, they would provide around 13 grams of protein. Then, have a peanut butter sandwich for lunch. It has five grams of protein from one tablespoon of peanut butter and around seven grams from two slices of bread. That adds up to 25 grams of protein. And, you haven't eaten supper yet!

How much protein should you eat in a day? If you are between 7 and 10 years old, you should eat an average of 24 grams of protein each day. The word average is important! You don't need to eat exactly 24 grams of protein each day. For example, one day you may eat 40 grams of protein, while the next day you may only eat 20. Put those days together and divide by two, and you have averaged 30 grams of protein per day.

Some people may need a bit more protein than others. For example, adults have more body to replace and repair than children do. People who exercise a lot burn more **calories** and have more muscle to maintain. Even these increased needs, however, are usually met without too much extra effort.

Hot dogs are a source of protein, but they are also high in fat. So, remember to eat them in moderation.

Too Much

Your body has a very good way to get rid of extra protein. For this reason, you would need to eat more than twice the recommended amount of protein over a long period of time before appearing ill. Eating more protein than you need, however, has its drawbacks.

First, you may become **dehydrated**. Your kidneys have the important job of getting rid of extra protein. They require a lot of water to flush out protein waste in urine. This process is hard on your kidneys, and it steals a lot of your body's water to do the flushing.

Second, foods that are protein-rich are often high in saturated fat. Too much saturated fat is not good for your heart. In fact, foods such as cheese and steak are higher in fat than in protein!

Opposite page: The cafeteria at school is a good place to get a balanced diet. Schools work hard to provide children with items from each of the food groups.

Third, too much protein in your diet may mean other important food groups and their **nutrients** are being left out. And, eating too much protein may cause you to gain weight. That's because protein can't be stored in the body. Your body turns extra protein into body fat. This also happens to carbohydrates and fat from a big meal, so a balanced diet is important.

Too Little

Most people in the United States eat nearly twice the amount of protein their bodies need. On the other hand, people who are trying to lose weight or are sick may not be eating enough protein. This can also happen when a person eats more empty **calories** than **nutrient**-rich food.

Many children have lost their lives to kwashiorkor. They did not receive the nutrients or medical attention they needed.

In poor countries, protein **deficiency** is a major problem. Usually it occurs in children. As you know, children need protein to grow. In some countries, however, children have very little to eat, and protein-rich foods are not available. This causes poor growth and illness and is called kwashiorkor.

Understanding **nutrients**, such as protein, and how your body uses them is important. It helps you choose foods that have the best materials for growing, repairing, and rebuilding your body. Look to the **Food Guide Pyramid** to determine how much protein you should eat.

Remember that it is important to know where to find the most nutrients in each food group. Choosing foods rich in nutrients over empty **calories** and eating a variety of foods will help you feel your best. It will also help your body grow and stay healthy.

The Food Guide Pyramid

Glossary

amino acids - the building blocks of proteins. Amino acids are made of carbon, hydrogen, oxygen, and nitrogen. There are 20 kinds of amino acids in the human body.

calorie - the unit of measure for food energy.

deficiency - a shortage of substances needed to be healthy.

dehydration - the result of too little water. A person becomes dehydrated when the fluid used and lost is not replaced.

digest - to break down food into substances small enough for the body to absorb.

element - one of more than 100 basic substances from which all other things are made.

Food Guide Pyramid - a chart used to describe dietary guidelines for Americans.

nerves - clusters of cells that the body uses to send messages to and from the brain.

nutrient - a substance found in food and used in the body to promote growth, maintenance, and repair.

peptide bond - a chemical link between carbon and nitrogen.

polypeptides - chains of amino acids.

reaction - the combination of two or more substances that produce something new, such as energy.

tissue - a group or cluster of similar cells that work together, such as a muscle.

virus - any of a large group of infective agents that are capable of growth and multiplication in living cells, and that cause various diseases.

Saying It

amino - uh-MEE-noh
bacteria - bak-TIHR-ee-uh
collagen - KAH-luh-juhn
deficiency - dih-FIH-shuhn-see
dehydrate - dee-HI-drayt
enzyme - EN-zime
hemoglobin - HEE-muh-gloh-buhn
insulin - IHN-suh-luhn

keratin - KEHR-uh-tun
kwashiorkor - kwah-shee-AHR-kuhr
legume - LEH-gyoom
peptide - PEHP-tide
polypeptide - pah-lee-PEHP-tide
saturated - SAH-chuh-ray-tuhd
thyroid - THI-royd
tofu - TOH-foo

Web Sites

To learn more about the nutrient protein, visit ABDO Publishing Company on the World Wide Web at **www.abdopub.com**. Web sites about nutrition are featured on our Book Links page. These links are routinely monitored and updated to provide the most current information available.

Index